DRESSING A NATION
THE HISTORY OF U.S. FASHION

BUCKSKIN
DRESSES
and
PUMPKIN
BREECHES

Colonial
FASHIONS
from the
1580s
to the 1760s

KATE HAVELIN

TFCB
TWENTY-FIRST CENTURY BOOKS
MINNEAPOLIS

Dedication

For my nieces, Althea, Anna, and Olivia. Althea designs her own jewelry. Anna seeks out vintage clothes. Olivia likes the simple comfort of sweatshirts from her favorite baseball team. Each is finding her own beautiful style.

Front cover image: In the colonial era, Indian women typically wore buckskin dresses, often adorned with beading. This photograph of a Sioux woman from the early 1900s shows that the fashion survived long after colonial times.

Back cover image: Sir Walter Raleigh and his son, Wat, are shown wearing pumpkin breeches in this oil painting from 1602. Raleigh was an Englishman who explored what are now the states of Virginia and North Carolina. This European style of dress, including the pumpkin breeches, made its way across the ocean to the American colonies.

Page 3 image: This woman wears a gown with lace at the neckline and sleeves, common for wealthy women in colonial times. U.S. artist John Hesselius created this painting in 1750.

Copyright © 2012 by Kate Havelin

Twenty-First Century Books
A division of Lerner Publishing Group, Inc.
241 First Avenue North
Minneapolis, MN 55401 U.S.A.

Website address: www.lernerbooks.com

Library of Congress Cataloging-in-Publication Data

Havelin, Kate, 1961–
    Buckskin dresses and pumpkin breeches : colonial fashions from the 1580s to the 1760s / by Kate Havelin.
        p.   cm. — (Dressing a nation: the history of U.S. fashion)
    Includes bibliographical references and index.
    ISBN 978-0-7613-5887-9 (lib. bdg. : alk. paper)
    1. Clothing and dress—United States—History. 2. Dress accessories—United States—History. 3. Indians of North America—Clothing. 4. United States—History—Colonial period, ca. 1600–1775. 5. United States—Social life and customs—To 1775. I. Title.
GT607.H38 2012
391.00973—dc22   201101176

Manufactured in the United States of America
1 – MG – 7/15/11

CONTENTS

This illustration from the 1800s shows how American Indians dressed in colonial times and for many years afterward. The drawing shows Indians of eastern North America and the Great Plains dressed in fringed buckskin shirts and cloaks, feathered headdresses, and leggings.

Chapter One

INDIAN

ATTIRE

The story of American colonial clothing begins long before 1607, when 104 British colonists (settlers) landed in Jamestown, Virginia. The Jamestown colonists were the first British settlers in North America. They and later European colonists laid the foundations for a society that eventually became the United States. But the land the colonists came to in Virginia was already populated. The Powhatan Indians, and their ancestors, had been living in Virginia for thousands of years.

Centuries ago, before Europeans arrived, North America was home to about five hundred Indian nations. Historians think the North American Indian population, before European contact, was around 1 to 12 million people. America's fashion story starts with these Indians, or Native Americans.

DO IT YOURSELF

In most Native American groups, women were the clothing makers. They used animal skins to make dresses, shirts, leggings, and shoes. They made warm robes out of animal fur. Deer were common across North America, and many native groups made clothing from deerskin (also called buckskin). Depending on where they lived on the North American continent, native peoples also made clothing from the hides and furs of these animals:

- **bears**
- **buffalo**
- **foxes**
- **moose**
- **mountain goats**
- **rabbits**
- **seals**
- **sea otters**

Many native groups made clothing from the fibers of hemp, flax, cotton, and other plants. Women twisted the fibers into strands. They wove, knotted, and braided the strands into cloth. Sometimes they colored the cloth using plant-based dyes. By soaking goldenrod flowers or the bark of birch trees in water, people got yellow dyes. Plants such as pokeberry and madder supplied red dyes. Indigo plants gave people blue dye.

WHAT'S IN A NAME?

The Tuscarora people, originally of North Carolina, used fibers of the hemp plant to make cloth for shirts. Their name for themselves was Ska-Ru-ren, the Tuscarora term for "shirt-wearing people."

During the colonial era and for many years afterward, Indians of the Great Plains wore animal skin robes. The style is seen in this mid-1800s illustration of a Mandan Indian.

This photograph shows materials that Shawnees used to make clothing in colonial times. The needles are made of animal bone and antlers. The thread came from animal sinew. The animal furs and hides were sewn into warm garments.

Native women sewed with needles made of stone or animal bone. Thread came from plant fibers, strips of leather, and animal sinew (a tough, stretchy cord attached to an animal's muscle). Native Americans decorated their clothing with materials they found nearby. These decorations included:

- seashells
- beads made from shells, stone, or animal bone
- pearls from the shells of oysters
- animal teeth
- feathers
- quills from birds and porcupines

Native Americans of the colonial era used dyes made from plants and minerals. They dyed porcupine quills (above) many different colors and used them to decorate clothing.

BEADS, BELTS, AND BLING

ndians of eastern North America made beads out of white and purple clam shells. The Narragansett Indians called the beads wampum, which means "white shell" in their language. Wampum makers bored tiny holes in the beads, strung them together into long strands, and wove many strands together to make belts, such as the one shown below.

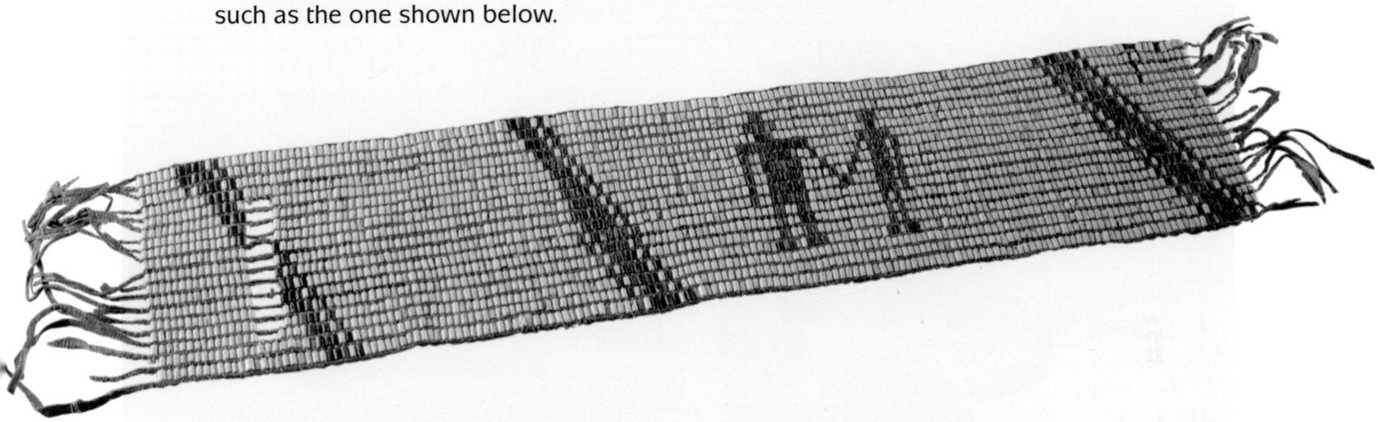

Some wampum belts held more than ten thousand beads. The patterns of the white and purple beads told stories and recorded tribal history. The colors of the beads also held meaning. White beads meant peace and health. Purple beads often signified grief. A wampum belt dyed red signaled war. Indians of different tribes gave wampum belts to one another to seal agreements or alliances. In 1682 William Penn, the English founder of the Pennsylvania Colony, made a treaty with the Lenni Lenape Indians. The Lenni Lenape gave Penn a wampum belt as a sign of goodwill. The belt shows two people—a native person and a white man—with hands joined in friendship.

The first Europeans in the Americas often traded with Indians. Both groups sometimes used wampum as money. In the mid-1600s, one 6-foot (2-meter) strand of wampum beads was worth about 10 English shillings (120 pennies). Purple beads were less common, so a string of purple wampum beads was worth twice as much as a string of white wampum.

BUCKSKIN BASICS

Although their cultures varied widely, most Indians in North America wore the same basic kinds of clothing. Most native men and some women wore breechcloths. The breechcloth, or loincloth, was a long piece of deerskin that wrapped between a wearer's legs. A belt held the cloth securely at the wearer's waist. Two long flaps draped down from the waist in front and back. Native men also dressed in buckskin shirts, leggings, vests, and coats.

This drawing by John White depicts a Native American man wearing a breechcloth, as well as traditional jewelry. White was an Englishman and artist who traveled to North America in the mid-1500s and painted watercolors of many Native American people.

THE BRAINY WAY TO MAKE BUCKSKIN

Across North America, native peoples hunted deer. They used every part of the dead animal. After hunters returned with their kill, people ate the deer meat. People used the bones of deer to make shovels, knives, scrapers, and other tools.

It was the women's job to turn deer hide into buckskin, or soft leather. First, women scraped all the hair from the hide using sharpened stones or animal bones. Next, they stretched the hide on a wooden frame and tacked it into place (as shown in the photo below from the early 1900s). They rubbed the hide with a solution made from water and the brains of deer. Chemicals in the brains softened and tanned the hide, turning it into leather (which will not decay the way rawhide will). Once the hide was soft and dry, women rubbed it with animal fat to make it even softer. Then they sewed the buckskin into shirts, dresses, breechcloths, and leggings.

Native women wore buckskin skirts, dresses, and sometimes leggings. A common outfit for women of the Great Plains—a vast region stretching from the Mississippi River to the Rocky Mountains—was the two-hide dress. It consisted of two deerskins sewn together with strips of leather, with openings for the wearer's head and arms. The dress had short buckskin sleeves, made from the hide of a deer's hind legs. A deerskin belt at the waist kept the dress fitted around the wearer's body.

Native clothing makers often trimmed the hems, sleeves, and cuffs of garments with deerskin fringe. The fringe served as more than just decoration. If a person got wet in a rainstorm or while wading through a stream, fringe absorbed the water from wet buckskin, helping it dry faster. Fringe also served as a kind of camouflage, or disguise. When seen from a distance, a person wearing fringe blended in with his or her background. This camouflage helped hunters approach animals without being noticed. It also helped people hide from human enemies. Native peoples often trimmed their everyday clothes with one layer of fringe, while garments for special occasions sometimes had many layers of fringe.

In this photo from the early 1900s, an American Indian woman wears some fashions that would have been worn by her colonial-era ancestors. These include a buckskin dress and shawl, a beaded belt, and braided hair.

A STUDENT'S BAG

Native Americans carried food, medicine, tools, and other gear in leather and cloth bags. One interesting example is a striped woolen bag from about 1650 *(shown at right)*. The gray-and-gold bag belonged to a young Wampanoag Indian, Caleb Cheeshahteaumuck. Caleb was about fifteen years old when he entered the Harvard Indian College. This was a school for Indian students at Harvard College (later Harvard University) in Cambridge, Massachusetts. Soon after graduating, Caleb died of tuberculosis, a lung disease. Twenty-first-century visitors can see his cloth bag at Harvard University's Peabody Museum.

Hundreds of years ago, long before the colonial era, Zuni people learned to grow cotton and weave it into cloth. This drawing from the mid-1800s shows a Zuni woman weaving on a loom.

Dressed for the Weather

Native clothing depended a lot on the weather. In warm places, many Indians wore very little clothing—only breechcloths for men and skirts for women. Women of the Timucua tribe of Florida wore fringed skirts or dresses made of Spanish moss, a soft, hairlike plant that drapes from the branches of trees. This outfit helped women stay cool in the steamy Florida heat. In the American Southwest, which can also be very hot, Zuni and Hopi peoples grew cotton plants. They wove the plant fibers into cloth and sewed lightweight cotton clothing. Some Native Americans didn't wear any clothes in warm weather.

In cold weather, Indian peoples wore coats, vests, and robes. On the Great Plains, which were home to millions of buffalo, people wore warm robes they made from buffalo fur. The Wampanoag people of Massachusetts wore warm capes crafted from the fur of:

- **raccoons**
- **otters**
- **beavers**

The capes draped over one shoulder and wrapped around the wearer's body. In the Great Basin, a desert region in the American West, people cut rabbit skins into narrow strips. They wove the strips together to make soft, warm capes.

In Arctic regions, the Inuit and Aleut peoples had to cope with extremely cold, harsh weather much of the year. They wore several layers of clothing, usually with a layer of soft, warm fur right next to their skin. The fur came from:

- **caribou**
- **seals**
- **polar bears**

Arctic peoples wore parkas, or hooded coats, with fur on the outside and a lining of bird feathers inside. The feathers trapped the wearer's body heat inside the coat. Arctic peoples also made gloves and socks out of animal fur. They made some clothing from the intestines of seals and walruses. The intestines were waterproof—so they kept people dry in wet and stormy weather.

Below right: During colonial times, and for many years before and afterward, Arctic peoples used animal furs to make warm clothing. This illustration shows a man wearing a fur parka, boots, and gloves.
Below left: An Arctic clothing maker made this tunic from the intestines of seals or walruses. Intestines are waterproof, so the garment would have kept the wearer dry.

ON YOUR FEET

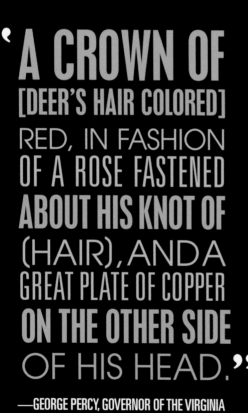

An Arctic clothing maker used seal and caribou skins, seal intestines, and wolverine fur to make these mukluks. The boots would have kept the wearer's feet and legs warm and dry. This style continued long after colonial times.

Moccasins, or deerskin slippers, were common footwear in most parts of North America. In Arctic regions, native peoples wore mukluks. These were boots made from sealskin or reindeer skin, lined with fur for extra warmth. In the deserts of the American Southwest, people needed to protect their feet from hot sand and sharp cactus needles. So they made sandals from yucca and other plant fibers. These shoes sometimes had deerskin soles, which made the shoes sturdier. In eastern North America, the Delaware Indians used corn husks to make lightweight summer moccasins. In places that were warm year-round, many native peoples went barefoot.

HIGH HATS

For special events, such as religious ceremonies, Native Americans often wore elaborate headdresses. The headdresses were fashioned from:

- **wood**
- **tree bark**
- **animal skins**
- **animal horns**
- **feathers**

Among the Iroquois, a group of six tribes in modern-day New York, headdresses showed a man's status within the community. Members of the Iroquois council, a governing body, wore deer antlers in their headdresses. If a member lost his position on the council, he had to give up his antlers. Many tribes along the East Coast made headdresses called roaches, which were worn into battle and for dances and religious ceremonies. Roaches were made from deer tails mixed with hair from moose and porcupines. A comb made from animal bone or

"A CROWN OF [DEER'S HAIR COLORED] RED, IN FASHION OF A ROSE FASTENED ABOUT HIS KNOT OF (HAIR), AND A GREAT PLATE OF COPPER ON THE OTHER SIDE OF HIS HEAD."

—GEORGE PERCY, GOVERNOR OF THE VIRGINIA COLONY, DESCRIBING THE HEADDRESS OF A POWHATAN CHIEF, CA. 1610

horn kept the roach in place atop a wearer's head. On the Great Plains, Crow warriors wore eagle feather headdresses into battle. The Crow believed that eagles gave their warriors great power. The Aleut people of western Alaska wore wooden visors. They steamed the wood until it was soft and could be bent into a curved shape. Then they decorated the visors with bright paint and the whiskers of seals or sea lions. In the Pacific Northwest, people made hats just like they made baskets, by weaving together plant fibers. The weavers used fibers of various colors to make pictures and patterns on the hats.

This visor was made of wood and decorated with paint, beads, and sea lion whiskers. In the colonial era, Aleut men wore this kind of hat while hunting sea animals. Visors kept the sun out of hunters' eyes and the rain and sea spray off their faces.

Masquerade

Many native peoples wore masks for special ceremonies. The Iroquois made masks from corn husks for their midwinter rituals. One group of Iroquois healers was known as the False Face Society. They made fantastical masks out of basswood. In spring and fall, members of the False Face Society put on their masks and walked through their villages. They performed rituals designed to get rid of spirits that were said to make people sick. Native peoples of the Pacific Northwest made wooden masks with inner and outer faces. The inner face was human. The outer face looked like an animal or spirit. The wearer could open and close the mask to change faces. This mask displayed people's belief that all humans and animals were connected.

Iroquois people of the colonial era wore different kinds of ceremonial masks. This one was made of woven corn husks.

NATIVE BABIES

Native American children often wore little or no clothing in warm weather. In cold weather, they dressed like their parents, in furs and buckskin outfits. In many tribes, mothers wrapped babies in deerskin and placed them in cradleboards. These were wooden frames covered with soft animal skins. A mother strapped a cradleboard to her back so she could carry her baby as she worked or traveled.

In wet regions where peat moss grows, native mothers used clumps of peat moss to diaper babies. Peat moss absorbs moisture like a sponge does. When a moss diaper was full, a mother tossed it out and replaced it with new moss.

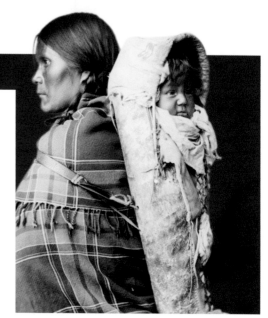

In the colonial era, an Indian woman might have carried her baby in a cradleboard on her back. This woman, photographed in the late 1800s, carries on the same tradition.

GOLD AND COPPER, PEARLS AND SHELLS

Native Americans wore jewelry for both decoration and identification. Certain items of jewelry told what family or tribe a person belonged to. Native peoples often wore jewelry for funerals, weddings, and other ceremonies. In battle, some western warriors wore necklaces made of grizzly-bear claws. These necklaces were believed to give warriors strength.

Jewelry traditions varied from place to place and depended on local resources. On the East Coast, some Indians wore necklaces made of deer hair that had been dyed red. The Timucua people of Florida wore earrings made from animal bone. The Algonquin of Virginia liked to fashion jewelry from pearls, which came from Virginia oysters. Other groups made jewelry from:

- **gold**
- **silver**
- **copper**
- **tin**
- **brass**
- **seashells**
- **tortoiseshell**
- **stone**

U.S. artist Charles Bird King made this painting of a Sauk Indian man in the early 1800s. Like his ancestors of colonial and precolonial times, the man wears an armband, earrings, and a necklace made from bear claws. He has decorative paint on his face and neck. His hair is wrapped up at the top of his head in a topknot.

HAIRDOS

Most native women wore their hair long, either loose or in braids. But some women wore distinctive hairstyles. For instance, young, unmarried Hopi women wore their hair in the squash blossom style. They wrapped their long hair around two wooden frames, one on each side of the head. The hair looked like two enormous, wide-open flowers above the wearer's ears. The style signified that the young woman was ready for marriage.

Most native men also wore their hair flowing loose or braided. But some sported topknots (hair knotted on top of the head), shaved heads, and other styles. Some men of the Mohawk tribe shaved their heads except for a strip of hair in the center, which ran from the forehead back to the neck. The men used bear grease to stiffen the hair, so it stuck straight up. In the Pacific Northwest, men sometimes wore mustaches and beards. But in most other places, native men were always clean shaven.

BODY *Art*

Many Native Americans painted their bodies using dyes made from plants and minerals. Some red and yellow dyes came from ocher, a kind of iron ore. White came from powdered limestone, chalk, or clay. Black came from charcoal and carbon.

Body paint protected people's skin from sun, wind, and bug bites. Black paint worn around the eyes cut down on glare from the sun or snow. Some natural dyes helped wounds heal. The colors and designs often

This painting by U.S. artist George Catlin, made in the mid-1800s, shows a Native American man wearing a roach. This kind of headdress was made of animal hair and feathers. This style was worn before, during, and after the colonial era. The man also wears jewelry and body paint.

held meanings. For instance, yellow, the color of the sun, was said to make wearers stronger. Warriors often painted their bodies and faces before battle, both to rally one another and to frighten enemies. On the Great Plains, both Blackfoot and Lakota warriors painted their faces black after a victory in battle. Among the Assiniboine tribe, also of the Great Plains, the chief painted his face yellow—which signaled his high status.

Before painting their bodies, people rubbed their skin with animal fat or grease. The grease made the paint look brighter and helped it wash off easier. People applied paint with their fingers or used the frayed ends of twigs as paintbrushes.

Some native groups used permanent tattoos for both fashion and tribal identification. They made tattoos by cutting designs into their skin and then rubbing ash into the cuts. To make different colors, they added vegetable or mineral dyes to the ash.

U.S. artist Henry A. Ogden made this drawing of the Jamestown settlement around 1900. The drawing shows Jamestown colonists building their settlement in 1607. Men wear pumpkin breeches, ruffled neck collars, stockings, and other attire typical of the early colonial period.

Chapter Two
DRESSING THE
COLONIAL MAN

Following the settlement at Jamestown in 1607, more Europeans came to North America. They formed small villages at seaports along the Atlantic coast.

At the beginning of the colonial period, in the early 1600s, France, Spain, Holland, England, and other European nations controlled different parts of North America. But through warfare and land deals, Great Britain gradually expanded its holdings in North America. By the end of the colonial period, in the 1770s, Britain controlled most of the eastern portion of the continent.

British territory was organized into thirteen colonies. The settlers who lived in the British colonies made many local laws. But they also had to follow British law.

PACKING FOR THE TRIP

Colonists crossed the ocean by boat, arriving in a "new world" that was very different from the one they had left behind in Europe. In the 1600s, most of North America was wilderness, without roads, farms, or cities. The newcomers from Europe had to start afresh. Everything they needed—from clothing to food to building materials—had to be shipped in from Europe, acquired from their Indian neighbors, or made by hand.

Most colonists came to America with only a small bundle of personal possessions, including a few items of clothing. In some cases, big British companies paid for settlers to travel to America. For instance, starting in 1628, the Massachusetts Bay Company sent groups of settlers to Massachusetts. On one voyage, the company provided the men in the expedition with clothing. Each man's allotment included:

- **four pairs of shoes**
- **four pairs of stockings**
- **four shirts**
- **two jackets**
- **one woolen cap**
- **two pairs of gloves**
- **one cloak**

Many women and children were on the same voyage. But either the company did not give them clothing or simply failed to write about it.

This painting shows British settlers arriving at Plymouth, Massachusetts, in 1620. The men wear hats with tall crowns, white collars, breeches, and cloaks. The women wear bonnets, long skirts, and cloaks. Children dress like the adults. W. J. Aylward made the painting in the late 1800s.

A MAN'S OUTFIT

The typical male colonist in North America wore knee-length trousers called breeches. They were made of many materials, including wool, leather, and cotton. Below his breeches, he wore linen or woolen stockings. These were knee-high knit socks, secured around his legs with bands or laces.

On his upper body, a man wore a long linen shirt with a drawstring or open collar at the neck. The long tails of the shirt tucked into the man's breeches. He covered the shirt with a waistcoat, which resembled a vest. Over his waistcoat, he wore another layer, either a short, close-fitting jacket or a longer frock coat.

English explorer Sir Walter Raleigh wears an elegant outfit, including pumpkin breeches, a short jacket, and a ruffled collar in this drawing from 1605. Raleigh and other explorers brought European styles to the American colonies.

PUMPED UP

Colonial American men sometimes showed off their physiques by padding their jackets and breeches with stuffing. The puffy pants were called pumpkin breeches. Colonists padded their clothes with:

- **rags**
- **horsehair**
- **sacks of grain**

Men claimed to pad their clothing for protection from enemy swords or arrows. But in reality, padded clothing was mostly about style. Puffy breeches made men's thighs look more muscular. Padded jackets made men's chests look big and strong. Shapely legs and broad chests were a key part of a man's good looks in colonial times. The fashion began in Europe and spread to America.

Pumped-up clothes could be a mess, however. If clothing ripped, the stuffing could spill out. The stuffing also attracted bugs and mold.

The coat reached almost to the knee. Most colonial men wore cravats around their necks. These were long pieces of white cloth that wrapped around the neck several times.

Colonial men wore woolen capes and coats in cold weather. Capes, also called cloaks, fastened at the collar with clasps, or hooks. They did not have sleeves but instead draped over the wearer's shoulders and arms. Greatcoats were heavy, knee-length overcoats.

Colonial men didn't wear modern-style underwear. The linen shirt that a man wore beneath his waistcoat and tucked into his breeches was his inner layer of clothing. It covered his torso and his backside down to his knees. Colonial men also slept in their linen shirts. They did not change into pajamas for bed.

LOUNGEWEAR

For relaxing at home, some wealthy colonial men wore banyans. These were loose, lightweight gowns worn over shirts and breeches. Some banyans were made from light and cool fabrics. Others were heavily quilted to keep the wearer warm.

ON THE JOB

Some wealthy colonial men dressed in velvet and satin garments. But most colonial men were farmers, craftspeople, and laborers. They worked hard and needed sturdy work clothing. They wore clothing made from durable fabrics such as leather, linsey-woolsey (a mixture of linen and wool), and Osnaburg (a coarse heavy linen). The basic workingman's outfit included:

- **a linen or woolen shirt**
- **coarse woolen stockings**
- **loose leather breeches**
- **a leather jerkin, or sleeveless jacket**
- **a leather apron**
- **low-heeled leather boots or shoes**

Different workers added their own variations to this basic outfit. Farmers often wore long pullover smocks over their shirts. Sailors and slaves wore long, loose linen trousers instead of breeches. Liverymen, who worked with horses and carriages, dressed in formal uniforms decorated with braids and trim. Some explorers and frontiersmen copied the clothing traditions of Native Americans. They wore buckskin vests, shirts, shoes, and leggings.

Some colonial men wore trousers instead of breeches. The sailor in this illustration from the late 1700s wears trousers and a short jacket.

This leather garment, dating to about 1560, is a jerkin. A colonial workingman would have worn the jerkin over a linen or woolen shirt.

OFF DUTY

When a colonial craftsman was done working for the day, he tucked one corner of his apron under his belt. This was a sign he was off duty.

Workingmen didn't wrap their necks in fancy white cravats. Instead, they wore dark-colored kerchiefs, or simple square clothes, around their necks. Kerchiefs were practical. Men used them to wipe sweat and dust from their faces. Dark-colored kerchiefs didn't show dirt the way white cravats did.

Servants and Slaves

About half of all Europeans in colonial America were indentured servants. They were too poor to pay their own way to America. So they made deals with landowners and business owners in the American colonies. These masters provided food, clothing, shelter, and transportation to America. In exchange, the indentured servant worked for the master's farm or business for four to seven years. When this period was over, the servant could live as a free person. Male indentured servants dressed like other working men in colonial America, in sturdy breeches, jerkins, aprons, and boots.

Many African slaves also lived in colonial America, mostly in the South. A slave was considered the property of his or her master. Slaves worked without pay. They had no rights or freedoms. Masters supplied slaves with

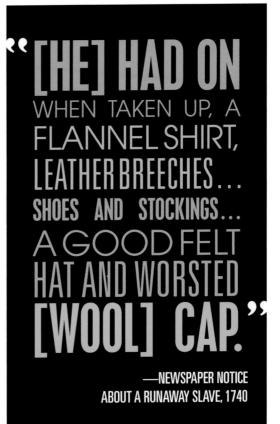

"[HE] HAD ON WHEN TAKEN UP, A FLANNEL SHIRT, LEATHER BREECHES... SHOES AND STOCKINGS... A GOOD FELT HAT AND WORSTED [WOOL] CAP."

—NEWSPAPER NOTICE ABOUT A RUNAWAY SLAVE, 1740

This drawing from the late 1700s shows slaves at work at Mount Vernon, the Virginia estate of future U.S. president George Washington. The slaves wear simple linen and woolen clothing—dresses for the women and shirts and trousers for the men.

food, shelter, and clothing, which was usually of the lowest quality. A field slave, who worked outdoors, got two suits a year—one for winter and the other for summer. For male slaves, the winter clothing allotment consisted of:

- **a woolen jacket**
- **a pair of woolen breeches or trousers**
- **two woolen shirts**

In summer, male slaves got lighter-weight breeches and shirts. The shirts were made of linen or cheap Osnaburg fabric. Jackets were made of cotton or wool. Male slaves who worked indoors, such as butlers and other house servants, dressed a lot like their masters. They wore linen stockings, breeches, shirts, waistcoats, and jackets.

CONVICTS IN AMERICA

In the 1600s, English prisons were overcrowded. At the same time, the American colonies desperately needed workers. England solved two problems at once by sending thousands of convicts to work for farms and businesses in North America. Under this arrangement, the convicts worked for no pay for a certain length of time. Their masters provided them with food, clothing, and shelter. In a long poem, English convict James Revel lamented his poor treatment at the hands of his master. Part of the poem describes his low-quality clothing:

> Where my Europian clothes were took from
>   me,
> Which never after I again could see.
> A canvas shirt and trowsers then they gave,
> With a hop-sack frock [smock] in which I
>   was to slave.
> No shoes nor stockings had I for to wear
> Nor hat, nor cap, both head and feet were
>   bare.
> Thus dress'd into the Field I nex[t] must go,
> Among tobacco plants all day to hoe.

Keeping It SIMPLE

Many Europeans came to North America so they could practice their religions freely. Such freedom wasn't allowed in much of Europe at the time. In Massachusetts many colonists belonged to the Puritan faith, a branch of Christianity. Puritanism stressed simplicity and strict religious devotion.

Puritans believed that fancy clothing was a sign of wickedness. In 1634 the Massachusetts

IN LIVING COLOR

People in colonial America often dressed in vibrant shades of blue, green, yellow, red, and orange. They learned to make plant dyes from their Native American neighbors. In Puritan Massachusetts, however, people mostly wore subdued colors. But red was still popular there, especially for men's coats and capes. The Quakers also preferred dark clothing, but Quaker men often wore bright green aprons. They also wore red cloaks, which they called cardinals, after the redbirds.

colonial government, which was headed by Puritans, outlawed garments adorned with:

- **silver**
- **gold**
- **silk**
- **lace**

In keeping with their religious beliefs, Puritan settlers did not adorn their clothing. They usually wore dark colors. This Puritan man dresses mostly in black. He wears a brown cape around his shoulders.

The Massachusetts government even had the authority to confiscate, or seize, clothing if it was considered too fancy.

The typical Puritan man dressed in dark colors, such as black, gray, and green. He wore the standard colonial man's outfit—cloth or leather breeches, woolen stockings, a linen shirt, and a waistcoat. Over his waistcoat, he wore a short, tight-fitting jacket called a doublet. Around his neck and shoulders, he wore a big stiff white collar, called a falling band, or a plain band.

Quakers also came to America for religious freedom. They were members of the Religious Society of Friends, a group that formed in England in the mid-1600s. A man named William Penn founded a Quaker colony in Pennsylvania in the 1680s. Like the Puritans, the Quakers preferred simple, unadorned clothing. They often wore subdued colors such as brown and gray. The typical Quaker man also dressed in the basic colonial outfit: stockings, breeches, a waistcoat, and a linen shirt. Over his waistcoat, he wore a simple frock coat, with little or no decoration at the cuffs and the collar. He typically wore a cravat around his neck.

Like the Puritans, Quaker settlers wore simple clothing and dark colors. This painting from around 1700 shows William Penn, founder of Pennsylvania, a Quaker colony. He wears a dark frock coat, waistcoat, breeches, stockings, and shoes.

DRESSING FOR SHOW

While Puritans and Quakers kept it simple, some colonial men, especially the wealthy, dressed in flashy and stylish clothing. Peter Stuyvesant was the governor of New Netherlands, a Dutch colony in modern-day New York. He wore caps, jackets, and breeches made of rich velvet. His shoes had big fancy rosettes, cloth decorations that resembled roses. His jackets had slashes in the sleeves. Slashes were openings that offered a glimpse of the layers of clothing underneath. Wealthy colonists such as Stuyvesant liked to show they were wearing inner layers of expensive linen and lace. Wealthy men also liked to wear fancy linen and lace collars and cravats to show off their status.

In this portrait from the 1600s, New Netherlands governor Peter Stuyvesant wears a large white collar and a gold sash at his shoulders. Stuyvesant often dressed in bright colors and flashy styles.

John Alden and Priscilla Mullens Alden came to Plymouth, Massachusetts, with the first English settlers in 1620. In this painting, Priscilla dresses typically for women in the colonial era. She wears a simple dress, a white apron, a short cape, and a plain bonnet. The painting was made by British-born artist George H. Boughton in the late 1800s.

Chapter Three

WOMEN'S AND CHILDREN'S WEAR

*L*ike men, women of the American colonies wore many layers of clothing. The inner layer was called a bedgown. It was a plain, knee-length linen dress. Over her bedgown, a woman wore a stay, later called a corset. This was a tight vest lined with reeds or strips of whalebone (stiff material from the jaws of whales). The stay tied with laces at the chest. Stays were supposed to improve a woman's posture.

On her legs, the typical colonial woman wore linen or woolen stockings. She covered these with several underpetticoats, or underskirts, usually made of linen or wool. Over these layers, she wore a dress or a gown. Working women wore simple dresses made of:

- **linen**
- **cotton**
- **wool**

Wealthy women wore gowns made of silk and satin. In cold weather, a woman might also wear a woolen cloak, a woolen hood, or a shawl made of animal fur.

WOMEN AT WORK

Colonial women often worked alongside their husbands on farms and in shops. Many cared for farm animals. Women made their family's soap, cheese, and butter. They hauled water from wells. Other household chores included cleaning, cooking, spinning yarn, sewing clothes, mending clothes, washing clothes, and caring for children. Like men, working women needed sturdy clothing. They wore simple fabrics like:

- **wool**
- **linsey-woolsey**
- **chintz (a shiny cotton)**

This colonial woman was probably very wealthy. Her gown is made of fine fabric. She wears a shimmery shawl over her shoulders, an elegant necklace, and a flower at her neckline. American artist John Singleton Copley painted her portrait in about 1763.

Working women often wore short gowns, or short jackets, over their dresses. They wore linen aprons to keep their dresses clean. They also wore simple, inexpensive kerchiefs to protect their necks from dirt, sun, and cold.

The colonial woman in this painting uses a knife to peel an apple. The apron that she wears over her dress protects it from spills and dirt.

DOUBLE DUTY

Like a man's long linen shirt, the colonial woman's bedgown served several purposes. It was a woman's inner layer of clothing—she wore no other underwear—as well as her sleepwear.

HAZARDOUS FASHIONS

Colonial Americans heated their homes with fireplaces and cooked over open flames. All this fire was a hazard for a woman with several layers of petticoats. Many women tucked the bottoms of their skirts into their waistbands when they worked near flames.

Slave women also wore simple clothing and simple fabrics. Those who worked in the fields wore shifts (knee-length linen underdresses), woolen or linen petticoats, cotton dresses, and linen or woolen short gowns. They did not wear stays or stockings and sometimes went barefoot. Those women who worked in the master's house dressed more formally. In addition to their basic dresses and petticoats, they wore stays, stockings, and aprons.

"**FINE PINK** COLOURED WORSTED (WOOLEN) STOCKINGS, **AND LEATHER** SHOES, AN OLD DARK BROWN QUILTED **PETTICOAT, CHECK'D APRON, A STRIP'D** CHESTER COTTON BEDGOWN, AND A BLACK **BEAVER HAT.**"

—DESCRIPTION OF THE CLOTHING OF A RUNAWAY FEMALE SERVANT IN VIRGINIA, 1752

This painting shows a southern plantation in the late 1700s. While a white overseer looks on, two slave women break up the soil with hoes. They wear simple cloth dresses and short gowns (short jackets). British-born architect and artist Benjamin H. Latrobe made the painting in the late 1700s.

Dress Up

Some wealthy colonial women owned countless beautiful gowns. They wore layers and layers of petticoats, as many as six at one time. The many petticoats made a woman's gown look fuller. Many gowns and petticoats were made of expensive fabrics imported from Europe and Asia. These fabrics included shimmery satins and brocade—a type of silk adorned with gold and silver designs. Gowns were often adorned with lacy ruffles at the collar and the sleeves.

A colonial woman's clothing depended, in part, on the fashions of her homeland. In the Spanish colony of Florida, wealthy women dressed for church in "black silk basquinas [petticoats] with little mantillas [black lace veils] over their heads," just like the wealthy women of Spain. The Dutch brought a lace-making tradition to the Americas. Dutch women in America often wore gowns trimmed in lace.

This wealthy colonial woman, shown in a painting from 1748, wears a luxurious gown. It has a lace collar and cuffs, black ribbon, and other elegant details. Beneath the dress, a tightly laced corset gives the woman a tiny waistline.

STAY, STAY, STAY

Colonial people valued straight posture. They tried to stand upright, with chests out, shoulders down, and backs flat. All colonial women and some men wore stays to improve their posture. Colonists especially wanted girls to stand up straight and never slouch. Some parents tied wooden boards to girls' backs to straighten them. Even girls as young as two wore stays.

HOOPING STYLE

Following the styles worn in Europe, wealthy colonial women wore a framework of hoops beneath their gowns. The hoops were made of wood or metal. They had an oval shape, which made the wearer's gown flare out at the hips. Hoops gave gowns a wide bell shape, which also made the wearer's waist look smaller. Some skirts were so wide that women couldn't fit through doorways or into carriages.

Although they were fashionable, bulky skirts had many drawbacks. They made it hard for women to move freely. Colonial women were supposed to stay close to home, and big hoopskirts made sure they did. On the positive side, hoopskirts increased a woman's personal space—giving her a safe distance from unwanted advances by men. It was hard to get too close to a woman wearing a hoopskirt. In 1747 a colonial man named Robert Campbell called hoopskirts "a Fence to keep us [men] at an awful Distance."

I DO

Modern brides usually wear white, a symbol of purity. But that wasn't the style for colonial brides. Since white cloth is hard to keep clean, most colonial women wore colorful wedding dresses. They also wore the same dresses after their wedding days, on additional special occasions.

The woman in this oil painting wears a framework of hoops beneath her dress. They give the gown a wide bell shape. The portrait was made by British-born painter Joseph Blackburn in 1759.

This painting shows future U.S. president George Washington marrying Martha Dandridge Custis (center) in 1759. Like most colonial brides, she wears a colorful dress. The painting, by Junius Brutus Stearns, was part of a mid-1800s series showing major events in George Washington's life.

Many American colonists carried on the wedding traditions of their home countries in Europe. For instance, Dutch brides in New Netherlands topped their wedding outfits with crowns adorned with silver and jewels—real ones if the family was rich, fake ones if it was poor.

COLONIAL BABIES

Colonial mothers wrapped newborn babies tightly in long pieces of linen, a practice called swaddling. Adults thought that swaddling would help babies grow straight and tall. Mothers sometimes hung their swaddled babies from hooks on the wall. That way, a mother could work while her baby slept. Colonial babies wore cloth diapers called clouts, which were fastened together with straight pins.

When babies got older, parents dressed them in dresses, petticoats, and aprons, often decorated with lace and flowers. The outfit was similar for boys and girls. Boys' dresses had sleeves with wide cuffs. The dresses buttoned in front, like long coats. Girls' dresses had narrow cuffs and fastened in back. Baby girls wore caps with ribbons. Baby boys wore caps with cockades, or badges.

Many toddlers wore a hat called a pudding cap, so named because it resembled a round dish used to serve pudding. Pudding caps were padded with extra cloth. The padding protected toddlers' heads when they fell as they learned to walk.

This painting of a mother and an infant from the 1670s shows the style for babies in the colonial era. Both boy and girl babies wore dresses, petticoats, aprons, and caps. The child in this painting is a girl.

Colonial mothers often sewed cords or strings to the shoulders of their toddlers' clothes. Parents held the strings while wobbly toddlers practiced walking. The strings also kept older toddlers from wandering off. Parents used hanging sleeves in the same way. These were loose sleeves with lots of ribbons and lace hanging from them. A parent could grab hold of a hanging sleeve to control an unruly child.

DRESSED LIKE
THEIR PARENTS

Sometime between the age of four and eight, colonial boys switched from wearing dresses to wearing breeches. Breeching—getting a first pair of breeches—signaled that a boy was becoming a man. By the age of eight or so, all colonial boys and girls dressed like adults. Boys wore breeches, stockings, waistcoats, and neck cloths. Girls wore petticoats and short coats.

In the mid-1700s, some Europeans began to condemn the tradition of dressing children like miniature adults. They thought children should have looser clothing, which would allow them to run and play. Christian Augustus Struve, a doctor in London, England, said, "The dress of children should be different than that of adults. It is disgusting to behold a child disfigured by dress, so as to resemble a monkey rather than a human creature."

For much of the colonial era, boys dressed just like their fathers. This young man wears a frock coat, a waistcoat, breeches, stockings, buckled shoes, and a neck collar. The painting was made around 1758 by American artist Joseph Badger.

SAMPLERS: ART AND INDUSTRY

All colonial girls learned needlework, the art of sewing and embroidering. It was an essential skill in colonial times, since stores did not sell ready-made clothing. Wealthy people could have their clothing custom made by tailors and dressmakers. But in most households, girls and women had to sew, weave, and knit clothing and bedding for the whole family.

To practice sewing, colonial girls made samplers *(a modern reproduction shown at right)*. Samplers are pieces of fabric decorated with basic and fancy sewing stitches. Using colored silk or cotton thread, girls stitched their samplers with names, rhymes, and the alphabet, as well as pictures of flowers and animals. Sometimes mothers ripped a daughter's sampler on purpose, so the girl could practice mending tears in cloth.

Around 1653 Loara Standish created the first American-made sampler. Loara was the daughter of Miles Standish, a leader of the Plymouth Colony in Massachusetts. In colonial times, families often displayed finished samplers on their walls. In modern times, colonial-era samplers are highly prized. One sampler, made by eleven-year-old Mary Russell in 1791, is valued at more than $200,000.

In response to such criticism, children's clothing began to change in both Europe and America. Boys started to wear open-collared shirts instead of neck clothes. They wore long trousers instead of breeches. Girls stopped wearing short coats, stays, and layers of skirts like their mothers. Instead, girls wore simple gowns with high waists and short sleeves. The loose-fitting dresses made moving easier.

Late in the colonial era, children stopped dressing like miniature adults. This painting from 1805 shows the new styles. Instead of breeches, the boy wears trousers. He wears an open-collared shirt instead of a neck cloth. The girl wears a loose, high-waisted dress rather than a corseted gown and petticoats.

This young man, painted by Benjamin West in the 1760s, is cleanly shaven. He wears his hair below his ears. His look is typical of men of the colonial era.

Chapter Four
ACCESSORIES:
FROM HEAD TO TOE

From head to foot, hair and accessories were important details for American colonists. As with their clothing, colonists followed European trends. For example, early in the colonial era, some American men wore mustaches and neatly trimmed, pointed beards, which were fashionable in Europe. But by the 1700s, facial hair had fallen out of fashion in both Europe and America.

In many colonies, men let their hair grow long. They let it drape over their shoulders or pulled it back into a neat pigtail. Massachusetts was the exception. The Puritan men there wore short hair, cut in a bowl shape. This style earned them the nickname Roundheads. The short haircut was in keeping with the Puritan emphasis on simplicity. The Puritan Plymouth Colony even had laws forbidding men from wearing long hair.

Wiggy Fashions

In the mid-1600s, men in Europe began wearing wigs made of human, horse, or goat hair. The craze started with French king Louis XIII (1601–1643). He wore a wig to cover his balding head. Soon wealthy men in Europe and the American colonies were also donning wigs. Many men had more than one wig. Even some wealthy colonial boys wore wigs.

Like many well-to-do colonial men, Charles Calvert, governor of the Maryland colony in the late 1600s, wore a showy wig. British artist Godfrey Kneller painted this portrait of Calvert.

Wigmakers sold wigs in dozens of styles. Some wigs had curls. Others were bushy. Some had braided tails in the back. Most wigs were covered in gray or white powder. Those who could afford the biggest and fanciest wigs were called bigwigs.

Wearing a wig took some effort and attention. Wigs fell off easily, so men practiced walking slowly to keep their wigs securely on their heads. Wigs were hot, so many men shaved their heads to stay cooler. A man wearing a wig often carried his hat rather than perching it awkwardly on his big wig. Men even had to worry about wig snatchers, thieves who stole wigs off men's heads when they were walking outside.

Wigs were popular throughout the colonies But in Puritan Massachusetts, wigs were barely tolerated. In 1675 a Massachusetts court declared that wigged men looked too much like women. A well-known Puritan minister, Increase Mather, called wigs "horrid bushes of vanity."

This painting shows Puritan colonists landing in Plymouth, Massachusetts, in 1620. The young man on the left wears a bowl-shaped haircut—a style that led to the nickname Roundheads.

BIG HAIR

A woman's hairstyle in colonial America depended a lot on her status. Colonial women often grew their hair long, past their shoulders, but they didn't let it hang loose. Most colonial women pulled it back from their faces and tucked it inside caps or bonnets. They let only a few curls or ringlets show in front. To display more hair would have been considered immodest.

This colonial mother wears her hair in the tower and commode style, which involved wrapping the hair over a big wire frame. The style went out of fashion in the late 1700s. Benjamin West made the painting of the woman and her children.

Meanwhile, many wealthy women embraced the tower and commode hairstyle that was popular in France at the time. To create this hairdo, a woman perched a tall wire frame on her head. She wrapped and piled her own long hair over the frame. She then attached hairpieces (made of animal or human hair) to the pile, making it even bigger. Some hairdos towered 12 inches (30 centimeters) above a woman's head. Curling and styling these big arrangements sometimes took several hours and required the assistance of servants. Colonial women used animal fat or a paste of flour and water to hold their big hairdos in place, the way modern women use hairspray.

By the late 1700s, the tower and commode style was passé. Following fashion trends in Great Britain, American women switched to the low hair style. Instead of creating elaborately fashioned piles of hair, they curled or braided their long hair and pinned it neatly on top of their heads.

THE COLONIAL COMPLEXION

Like modern women, colonial women wanted smooth and fresh-looking skin. Among wealthy women, a pale complexion was highly prized. It was a sign that a woman didn't need to labor outdoors or over a hot fire like a servant or a slave. Some young women wore linen masks in summer to protect their faces from the sun.

Some colonial women made their own makeup. Using recipe books, they mixed together ingredients such as:

- **beeswax**
- **animal fats**
- **nut oils**
- **spices**
- **flour**
- **cornstarch**

They used vegetable dyes to make red lipstick and green or blue eye shadow. They rubbed dye made from rose petals onto their cheeks for a rosy glow.

CHEEK
PLUMPERS

Many colonial Americans had rotten teeth. Unlike modern Americans, they didn't visit dentists for regular cleanings. Fluoride toothpaste hadn't been invented. As a result, many people's teeth decayed and fell out when they were still young adults. People who had lost teeth were often left with hollow cheeks. For a more natural look, some colonists inserted small cork balls into their cheeks. These plumpers rounded out their hollow cheeks, giving the appearance of a mouth full of teeth.

This colonial woman, painted in 1720, wears makeup to redden her cheeks and lips. American artist Geradus Duyckinck made this portrait.

Covering Up

Many colonists were disfigured by smallpox, which was very common at the time. This contagious disease causes high fevers and severe blisters, or pox. The disease is often deadly. People who survived smallpox were usually scarred for life. The skin on their faces was left with pockmarks, or small pits. Both men and women wore makeup to cover pockmarked skin. They made white face powder from flour, ground rice, chalk, or cornstarch.

Many women wore beauty patches to cover pockmarks. These were small bits of paper, shaped like:

- **hearts**
- **clubs**
- **diamonds**
- **spades**
- **flowers**

Beauty patches became quite popular. In fact, some colonial women wore beauty patches just for decoration, not to cover up pockmarks.

TO TOP IT OFF

American colonists wore hats all the time, even inside. At home, women wore simple linen caps called coifs. These hats had strings in the back to keep them securely on the wearer's head. Coifs protected women's hair from soot from the fireplace and other household dirt. When a woman went out, she wore another hat over her coif. Puritan and Quaker women wore simple cloth bonnets. Some wealthy women wore big hats called calashes. Typically made of silk, with a frame of thin wooden sticks, these hats were big enough to cover a large hairdo. Many women's hats sported decorative:

- **feathers**
- **ribbons**
- **flowers**
- **bows**

Top: A colonial mother wears a calash in this painting from the mid-1700s. The big hat covers her big hairdo.
Left: Puritan, Quaker, and other colonial women often wore simple cloth bonnets when they left the house.

THE OLD PLANTATION

In the late 1700s, one South Carolina slave owner made a watercolor painting of his slaves. *The Old Plantation (right)* shows a dozen slaves gathered outside, dancing and playing music. One slave plays a banjo. Another plays a drum. All the slaves are barefoot and wear colonial-style clothing—waistcoats and breeches for men and simple dresses for women. Several of the slaves have kerchiefs wrapped around their heads. The head wrap was a distinctively African American style in colonial times.

CRAZY FOR BEAVER FUR

When Europeans arrived in North America, they discovered that the continent was home to millions of beavers. They also discovered that beaver pelts made high-quality hats *(right)*. Beaver fur is waterproof, and when made into a hat, it holds its shape better than any other animal fur. Back in Europe, the demand for beaver pelts exploded. Indian and European trappers killed beavers by the tens of thousands. European merchants imported vast quantities of beaver pelts for hat making.

The beaver hat craze took its toll on European hatters, the people who made the hats. To make beaver fur into hats, hatters used mercury, a silvery white metallic liquid. In the process, they sometimes inhaled poisonous mercury fumes. Those who inhaled too many fumes got sick. They couldn't talk, walk, or think properly. In modern times, the phrase "mad as a hatter" describes someone who's not in his or her right mind. The term originates with European hatters who lost their senses due to mercury poisoning.

At one time, North America was home to about 60 million beavers. But because of the craze for beaver fur hats, the animals were hunted nearly to extinction. By 1900 almost all the beavers in North America had been killed. The beaver population has since increased.

Some workingmen wore simple wide-brimmed hats made of wool, straw, or cloth. Many sailors, slaves, and other workingmen wore knitted woolen caps. In Massachusetts, Puritan men wore felted (matted) beaver fur hats with steep crowns, or tops. Quaker and Dutchmen wore hats with wide, upward curving brims and low crowns. Many wealthy men wore tricornes, a style that was also popular in Europe. These hats had a wide brim that was turned up, or cocked, on three sides. The fanciest tricornes had silver or gold trim.

The tricorne hat was a common style for colonial-era men. The hat's broad brim was turned up on three sides.

STEPPING OUT IN STYLE

Wealthy colonial men wore shoes made of soft leather. Shoemakers dyed the leather to suit a customer's preference—black was the most common color. Men's shoes normally fastened with shiny silver buckles. The heels might be high or low, depending on current fashions. For a time, square toes were popular. Late in the colonial era, pointed toes came into style.

Wealthy women wore shoes made of leather, silk, satin, and other rich fabrics. These shoes also had high or low heels, depending on current fashions. Many had sharply pointed toes. They fastened with buckles or clasps. They were often decorated with:

- **lace**
- **trim**
- **bows**

These high-heeled shoes from the 1600s are made of leather and silk. The toes are sharply pointed. The wearer was probably a wealthy colonial woman.

Shoes normally had leather soles and wooden heels. But some very rich colonists wore shoes with paper soles. The thin soles demonstrated that a person didn't have to work, walk, or even stand a lot. He or she traveled by carriage and had servants to do household chores.

WORK *Shoes*

Ordinary people needed practical footwear. Working people, both men and women, wore simple, sturdy leather shoes that fastened with ties or buckles.

Colonial roads were unpaved. They were rutted, muddy, and filled with animal manure. Outdoors, some people wore clogs called pattens, or goloe-shoes. These were tall platforms that attached to ordinary shoes. They raised the wearer up above the mud.

ALL THAT GLITTERS

Many wealthy colonial women loved jewelry and wore:

- **pearl necklaces**
- **gold pendants**
- **diamond earrings**
- **silver bracelets**

They pinned up their hair with gold and silver bodkins, a type of hairpin. One Virginia plantation owner listed among his household possessions: "a sapphire set in gold, one ring with a blue stone,

This colonial woman was probably well to do, as shown by her pearl necklace and the jewels in her hair, as well as by her fur-trimmed gown. This portrait was painted by John Singleton Copley in 1763.

another with a green stone, and another still with a yellow stone . . . a diamond ring . . . and an amber necklace."

For men, buttons were a form of jewelry in colonial times. On cloaks and waistcoats, some wealthy men wore big silver buttons engraved with their initials. Some very rich men used real silver dollars as buttons. Some wealthy Dutch colonists used gold and precious stones as buttons.

> "A WOMAN'S FAN; A GOLD NECKLACE . . . PLAIN GOLD RING. SETT OF GOLD SLEEVE BUTTONS, GOLD LOCKET, SILVER HAIR PEG, SILVER CLOAK CLASPS, AND A STONE BUTTON SET IN SILVER."
> —PORTION OF A LIST OF A CONNECTICUT WOMAN'S POSSESSIONS UPON HER DEATH, 1757

Puritan and Quaker women did not wear jewelry, however. To do so would have violated their commitment to modesty and simplicity. Many working-class colonists wore no jewelry simply because they couldn't afford it. Some slaves and servants wore homemade jewelry. Both slave men and women wore earrings made of:

- **animal bone**
- **beads**
- **ivory**
- **copper**
- **brass**

American political leader John Hancock wears a jacket with ornate buttons in this portrait by John Singleton Copley from the late 1700s.

This fan from the mid-1700s was made of ivory (expensive material from the tusks of an elephant or other animal), with a covering of richly painted paper.

Fantastic

For wealthy and fashionable colonial women, a fan was a key accessory. Women carried fans to parties and dances. They used them to cool themselves on hot summer days and also fluttered them flirtatiously at male suitors. Fans were made of:

- **paper**
- **silk**
- **lace**

They were set on a framework of bamboo sticks, carved wood, or ivory. When spread open, some fans revealed words or pretty pictures. Others had fancy decorations.

HOLDING THE BAG

Most colonial clothing didn't have pockets. So where did people stash their stuff? Workingmen carried knives, tools, and other gear in haversacks, large leather or cloth bags that they slung over their shoulders. Wealthy men stored their extras—things like pipes, pocket watches, and snuff (tobacco) boxes—in leather pouches. They tied the pouches to their belts.

Colonial women tied cloth bags or small leather cases to the waistbands of their skirts. The bags were often elaborately decorated with lace, needlework, and silk flowers. They held handy items such as thimbles, scissors, and tiny vials of perfume.

BLACK *and* GRAY

When death came in the colonial era, living people changed their clothes. Family and friends wore black, a sign of mourning. Some wealthy families even outfitted their servants and slaves in black clothing. Men's mourning clothes didn't have any buttons, which were considered to be decorative and therefore not in keeping with the somber mood. People in mourning wore black bands around their hats. Close relatives wore mourning clothes for months or years. As time passed after a death, people switched to lighter colors, such as gray or purple.

Many colonists wore mourning rings, lockets, and brooches, engraved with the dead person's name, age, and date of death. Some mourning jewelry had a small compartment for holding a lock of the dead person's hair.

These are mourning lockets, decorated with pictures of or memorials to someone who has died. In colonial times, family members wore such lockets to honor dead relatives.

Americans of the colonial era wore dark mourning clothing after the death of a loved one. This widow wears a dark dress and a black shawl. John Singleton Copley made her portrait in 1766.

This painting from the mid-1700s shows a colonial woman reading a book while she spins. Her spinning the wheel turns raw wool into yarn, which will then be woven into cloth.

Chapter Five

THE CLOTHING SUPPLY

Centuries ago, sewing and knitting were not just hobbies. They were necessary skills for women. In both colonial and Native American societies, women were responsible for making much of a family's clothing. Native American girls learned to tan deerskin and other animal hides. Native women also sewed and decorated clothing. All colonial girls learned to sew. They became expert at making everything from linen shirts to wool petticoats. They also knitted stockings and gloves. This work took skill and patience.

Women spent countless hours spinning wool, sewing, and mending. They worked at home, in houses that were often poorly heated. Many colonial women wore mitts, or fingerless gloves, while they worked. Mitts kept a woman's hands warm but still allowed her to do precise work with her fingers.

Making clothes, washing them, and mending them were ongoing jobs. Clothes ripped and wore out. Clothing that didn't fit anymore had to be remade. Fabric was expensive to buy and time consuming to make, so colonists saved and used every scrap. They handed down outfits from older to younger children. When clothing was too worn to repair, women used the scraps as rags or sewed many small scraps together into quilts and rugs. They even reused old buttons. Slave women sometimes made children's clothing from old sheets.

Colonial women created new clothing from scratch and also mended and altered existing garments. This woman is either making or repairing a dress.

A BLUE STORY

In the 1730s, a young woman named Eliza Lucas Pinckney found a way to improve indigo dye. This clear blue dye comes from the indigo plant. Colonists, especially those in the South, used indigo to color clothing and other textiles. Unlike many girls in colonial America, who did not go to school, Pinckney had attended school. Her favorite subject was botany, the study of plants.

Pinckney was just sixteen years old when she took over her family's three South Carolina plantations. Her mother couldn't help run the plantations because she was ill. Pinckney's father was a colonel with the British army. He was stationed on the island of Antigua in the Caribbean Sea.

Pinckney wanted to grow a new crop that would make the family plantations profitable. She began planting indigo seeds that her father had sent from Antigua. She experimented by crossbreeding seeds from different indigo plants. With the help of slaves, she developed a plant that yielded high-quality blue dye.

Her plants were a big success. Soon European clothing makers were demanding South Carolina indigo dye. It became the most popular dye in Europe and the second-biggest cash crop in South Carolina.

A colonial woman scrubs clothing in a washtub. Before starting this task, she had to haul water from a river or a well and heat it on the stove.

LOADS OF LAUNDRY

Keeping clothes clean in colonial America was also hard work. Washing machines and clothes dryers didn't exist. People didn't even have running water in their homes. To do the wash, first a woman had to lug water home from a well or a nearby river. She had to make a fire and heat the water in a big pot. She boiled the dirty clothes, scrubbed them with homemade soap, rinsed them, and hung them indoors or outdoors for drying. Once the clothes were dry, the woman pressed them with a flat piece of iron that had been heated over a fire.

THAT'S NO LYE

The toughest part of cleaning clothes was making the soap. Most women made their own. They mixed fat or oil with lye (below), a strong solution made from ashes. Lye can sting and damage the skin, so soap making was an unpleasant task.

SMELLS GOOD TO ME

Colonial Americans didn't bathe much. As with washing clothing, taking a bath involved hauling pails of water to the house, heating it over the fire, and dumping it into a big tub. This was a lot of work, and people didn't do it often—only a few times a year. Some doctors even warned that bathing was bad for people's health.

Without regular baths, colonial people were smelly. Their clothes and bodies picked up odors from sweat, animals, and smoky fireplaces. To mask the odors, people used perfumes and powders. Both men and women carried pomanders *(right)*. These were small cases with tiny holes or other openings. People filled pomanders with fragrant mixtures of plants such as:

- **cloves**
- **orange blossoms**
- **rosemary**
- **pine needles**

The pleasant scents wafted out of the pomanders onto people's bodies and clothing.

Considering how much work was involved, it's not surprising that early colonists cleaned most of their clothes only a few times a year—about once every three months. Colonists cleaned linen shirts a bit more frequently, because dirty linen wore out faster than clean linen. In the 1700s, colonists did laundry a little more often—about once every two months. Certain fabrics, such as velvets and brocades, would shrink or lose their luster if they were washed, so women just spot-cleaned these fabrics with vinegar or white wine.

This drawing shows a tailor's workshop in the mid-1700s. Wealthier colonial men and women could afford to have tailors or sempstresses make their clothes.

A JOB FOR PROFESSIONALS

Not all the clothes in colonial America were homemade. Some people could afford to have their clothes made for them. Tailors were men who made fitted clothing, including coats, breeches, waistcoats, and jackets for men. They sometimes also made dresses for women. The first two English settlements in America, Jamestown and Plymouth, each had one tailor. Tailors had the tools to take precise measurements and to make clothing that fit a customer specifically. Some women also got paid for making clothes. A woman who sewed dresses or other clothes was called a sempstress or a mantua maker (a mantua was a loose-fitting gown).

It was expensive to have a tailor or sempstress sew custom-made clothes. For the most part, only the rich could afford it. To have an outfit tailor made, the customer first ordered a kit of materials from Europe. The kit included everything needed to make an outfit, including:

- **fabric**
- **trim**
- **buttons**
- **knee bands**

The customer took the kit to a tailor or sempstress, who then did the measuring, fitting, and sewing.

GONE BUGGY

Colonial people stored clean clothes in wooden chests. They scattered pine needles around the garments to keep them smelling fresh. But in the days before screen doors and tightly built houses, fleas, lice, and bedbugs often got into people's homes. The bugs sometimes infested chests full of clothing.

GEORGE AND MARTHA

The wealthiest Americans preferred to have British tailors make their clothing. Landowner and colonial legislator George Washington (later the first president of the United States) often ordered his clothes from a tailor in London. He once asked for a fashionable greatcoat that would fit a man who was about 6 feet (1.8 m) tall. But getting clothes made an ocean away was tricky. Sometimes it took a year to get a coat or other garment from Britain. And when the British-made clothing arrived, it didn't always fit.

"MY CLOATHES HAVE NEVER FITTED ME WELL."
—FUTURE U.S. PRESIDENT GEORGE WASHINGTON, 1761

Martha Washington, George's wife, wanted her clothes to fit precisely. So Martha's dressmaker in London had a mannequin, or dummy, made exactly in Martha's shape. By making clothes that fit the mannequin, the dressmaker assured a perfect fit for Martha. Martha also had her London dressmaker sew the latest-style dresses using cheap fabric. The dressmaker then sent the cheap dresses, along with fancy fabric, to the Washingtons' home in Virginia. There, Martha had American dressmakers use the cheap dresses as a guide. They sewed new ones in the same style using the better fabric.

George and Martha Washington, shown here with Martha's two children from a previous marriage, ordered custom-made clothing from tailors and dressmakers in London.

These wealthy colonial Americans wear fashions that were also popular in Europe at the time. The man's stylish attire includes a wig and a gold-trimmed waistcoat. The woman wears an elaborate gown and jewelry while the baby wears a silky gown. American artist Charles Willson Peale made this painting in the late 1700s.

BRINGING EUROPE TO AMERICA

Unlike the Washingtons, most colonists could not afford to work with London tailors and dressmakers. But colonists still wanted the latest styles from Europe. No one published fashion magazines in the colonial era. However, colonists got letters from friends and family in Europe, with descriptions of new fashions. Some wealthy colonists traveled back to Europe regularly. They bought new clothes, brought them back to America, and showed them off at parties.

Clothing makers who had worked in Europe were held in high regard. In an advertisement in a Philadelphia, Pennsylvania, newspaper, John Marie boasted that he was a "Taylor from Paris" and that he had "had the pleasure of pleasing some of the most respectable gentlemen in London."

Paris, France, was the center of style in this era, and wealthy colonists looked there for fashion cues. Judith Bayard, colonial governor Peter Stuyvesant's wife, was a Dutchwoman, but she "followed the French fashions in dress, displaying considerable artistic skill in the perfection and style of her attire." One portrait from the late 1600s shows Bayard dressed in an ornate lacy headdress, a dark gown with puffy lace ruffles at the sleeve, and a showy necklace and bracelets.

Fashion Babies

European styles also came to America via dolls called fashion babies. The dolls stood about 24 inches (61 cm) tall. Each month, dressmakers

This doll is a fashion baby. It would have been shipped from Europe to America, as a model for an American sempstress in sewing clothing for her wealthy colonial customers.

in London and Paris sent fashion babies to American sempstresses. The dolls were outfitted in miniature garments based on styles worn in Europe. Their hair was also done in the newest styles. The fashion babies showed American sempstresses how to make stylish clothes for their own customers. When the next set of dolls arrived from Europe, sempstresses sold the old ones.

SHOE SHOPPING

American colonists had a number of choices when it came to shoes. Most villages had cobblers, or shoemakers. They made shoes to fit specific customers and also repaired broken shoes. Some cobblers specialized in riding boots or women's shoes. A few shops made shoes in standard sizes and sold them ready-made. Some merchants imported and sold ready-made shoes from Great Britain.

While wealthy people spent lavishly on stylish buckled shoes, poor colonists had to economize. They wore and repaired the same pairs of shoes for years at a time. To make their shoes last longer, many people went barefoot in warm weather. Some poor people cobbled together their own homemade shoes. These rarely fit well.

This view from 1667 shows the harbor in New York bustling with activity. Ships from Great Britain brought cloth and many other goods to the American colonies.

EPILOGUE

In the early years of colonial America, most textiles came from overseas. Wealthy colonists bought imported fabrics, such as shimmery silk and nankeen cotton from China. Calico, a silky kind of cotton, came from Calicut, India.

Colonists also bought vast amounts of wool from England. The English government wanted Americans to keep buying English wool, not to spin their own wool and make their own woolen fabric. So in 1699, England passed the Wool Act. This law prohibited colonists from exporting American-made woolen goods. It said that colonists had to send raw wool back to England for processing. Other English laws said that Americans could import fabrics from China, India, and elsewhere only on English ships. All these laws were designed to keep profits from the textile business flowing to English merchants.

For many years, Americans obeyed British laws about clothing and imports. It made sense for them to import fabrics from Great Britain. For one thing, the colonies didn't have enough home-grown wool, cotton, and linen to dress their growing populations. One British ship could bring more cloth to America than the busiest American weaver could make in ten years.

But as the years passed, Americans grew angry with British laws. They wanted the freedom to make money as they pleased. They no longer wanted to support the British wool industry and other industries. They wanted to develop their own businesses. The cry went out for Americans to determine their own future.

INDEPENDENCE

In 1775 the American colonies went to war with Great Britain. The Revolutionary War lasted until 1783, when the United States won its independence. George Washington, a plantation owner, colonial legislator, and former military commander, became commander in chief of the Continental Army, America's fighting force. One of Washington's many decisions was what American soldiers would wear. The British troops had bright red military jackets, and people referred to the soldiers as redcoats. American soldiers needed their own uniform.

At first, Washington said troops should wear deerskin hunting shirts and "Indian Boots, or Leggins." He knew that deerskin clothes were cheaper and longer lasting than wool and cotton uniforms. Later, the colonies did establish a formal uniform. Each soldier was to get:

- **a blue coat**
- **a waistcoat**
- **four shirts**
- **four pairs of shoes**
- **four pairs of stockings**
- **two pairs of trousers**
- **a hat**
- **a hunting shirt**
- **a blanket**

But the colonies didn't have enough money to outfit everyone, so few soldiers got the full uniform. Some soldiers were forced to go without coats, shoes, or other basics. Officers wore basically the same clothing as enlisted men. To show their rank, officers wore colored ribbons across their chests, patches on their shoulders, and badges on their hats.

These Continental Army soldiers wear a basic uniform, including blue coats, white trousers, and waistcoats. But the army couldn't afford to supply every soldier with a complete uniform.

THE POLITICS OF **CLOTHES**

As part of the fight for independence, Americans rallied against British-made goods. Patriotic Americans encouraged their fellow colonists to boycott, or refuse to buy, British-made clothing. People began to wear homemade woolen and linen, called homespun.

Some colonists, such as statesman and inventor Benjamin Franklin, made a point of dressing plainly. In 1778 Franklin went to Paris on a diplomatic mission. Instead of wearing a fancy powdered wig, he wore a fur hat over his own gray hair. He wore a brown linen suit instead of formal velvets and brocades. Franklin was one of America's most famous men. His decision to dress like a homespun American sent a message to the world. In Paris, Franklin's clothes showed that America was a different kind of country. Although the powerful men of Paris wore wigs and stylish clothes, they liked Franklin's plain style.

On April 30, 1789, at his inauguration as the first president of the newly independent United States, George Washington set the tone for a new national style. The wealthy Virginia planter dressed in plain but elegant clothes. He wore a dark brown American-made suit and white shirt. The metal buttons on his waistcoat were engraved with eagles, a symbol of the new United States. He wore white silk stockings. Silver buckles gleamed on his black shoes. He wore his powdered hair tied back behind his head. He carried a sword, but he didn't wear furs or jewels. Washington didn't want to look like a pompous king.

When he visited Paris, France, in 1778, Benjamin Franklin *(center)* dressed simply, but he still impressed the famously fashionable French. Anton Hohenstein made this painting of Franklin's visit.

George Washington takes the oath of office as president of the United States in 1789. He wears a dark brown American-made suit. His accessories include a sword, buckled shoes, and a neck cloth.

SIMPLIFIED *Style*

As the nation moved forward, colonial fashions faded into the past. In the early 1800s, simplicity was the new watchword in American clothing. Men started wearing short riding jackets instead of knee-length coats. Breeches went out of style. All men switched to long trousers. Women's styles changed greatly too. For a time, women packed away their bulky hoopskirts. They switched to soft, clinging gowns with narrow skirts, high waistlines, and long tight sleeves. Instead of elaborate hairdos, they wore their hair in simple, loose curls.

THE MACHINE AGE

By the mid-1800s, the United States was in the midst of the Industrial Revolution. In many businesses, machines took the place of human laborers. Women still did needlework and sewed their families' clothing at home, but people also bought ready-made garments from clothing shops.

Mechanical looms and sewing machines could produce garments quickly and in vast quantities, far more than anyone could do by hand—and more cheaply.

In the early 1800s, bulky hoopskirts and petticoats went out of style. This woman wears a soft, Empire-style gown, with a high waist and narrow skirt. She wears her hair in loose curls.

In the mid-1800s, large manufacturers began to make cloth and clothing. In this illustration from 1834, women tend machines at a textile mill.

People who might have earned their living as shoemakers, dressmakers, and weavers in colonial times instead took jobs in textile mills, tending machines. Many colonial-era crafts and skills were lost. As the nineteenth century continued, clothing—and the way people made it, bought it, wore it, and cared for it—continued to change.

NO TURNING *Back*

In the twenty-first century, colonial-era clothing is the stuff of history lessons. Modern people wear powdered wigs and buckled shoes only at living history museums, such as Colonial Williamsburg in Virginia. Some historic reenactors dress up like Continental Army soldiers and put on mock battles with British redcoats. Other reenactors dress like colonial-era slaves, farmers, and craftspeople. Still, you're unlikely to see a man walking down the streets in knee breeches or a woman wearing layers of petticoats in the twenty-first century.

Colonial-era fashions might be long gone, but a few remnants survive in the English language. For example, we still call some people bigwigs, even though men don't wear powdered wigs anymore. We might say that someone's mad as a hatter—just like those hatters who lost their senses making beaver fur hats in the 1700s. And when we say that something's homespun, we mean that it's folksy and homemade, just like the cloth that colonial women wove and wore when they boycotted British wool. In modern times, we might not dress like colonial Americans, but their clothing traditions have left a mark on our culture.

1607 The first English settlers in North America land at Jamestown, Virginia. They bring small bundles of clothing with them.

early 1600s Wealthy men in Europe and colonial America begin wearing wigs, a style made popular by French king Louis XIII.

1634 Guided by Puritan teaching, the Massachusetts Bay Colony outlaws silk, lace, and other fancy fabrics.

late 1600s England passes a series of laws called Navigation Acts. The laws say that only English ships can bring silk, cotton, and other goods to the American colonies.

1653 Loara Standish of the Plymouth Colony sews the first sampler made in America. Colonial girls routinely stitched samplers to develop their needlework skills.

1675 A Massachusetts court condemns wigs for men, saying they make men look like women.

1699 England passes the Wool Act, which prohibits Americans from exporting woolen goods. The law is designed to protect England's wool manufacturers.

1730s Eliza Lucas Pinckney, who runs her family's South Carolina plantations, develops an improved indigo dye. It quickly becomes the most popular dye in Europe.

1760s Americans start to boycott British fabrics to protest British rule. They switch to wearing homespun linen and woolen clothing.

1775 The Revolutionary War begins, ending the colonial era in America.

brain tanning: treating raw animal hide with chemicals from an animal's brain. This process, called tanning, turns the hide into leather, which will not decay as rawhide will.

breechcloth: a long strip of deerskin or other material worn between the legs, with front and back panels that hang down from a band at the waist

breeches: tight, knee-length men's pants, with a band or buckles at the knee

brocade: a rich silk fabric with raised patterns made with gold and silver threads

buckskin: the tanned skin of a buck, or male deer. In colonial times, people often used the term *buckskin* to describe any clothing made of leather.

coif: a simple cloth cap worn by colonial-era women at home and under larger hats when they left the house. Coifs kept women's hair from getting dirty at home.

doublet: a short, close-fitting man's jacket, often worn over a waistcoat

embroidery: the art of stitching numbers, letters, designs, and other patterns on fabric with a needle and threads. People embroider clothing and other fabrics to enhance their beauty.

felt: fur or wool that has been formed into a stiff mat. People use heat, moisture, and pressure to create felt.

homespun: linen or woolen fabric made from yarn spun at home, by hand

hoopskirt: a woman's skirt with a frame of hoops underneath it, intended to give the skirt a wide bell shape

leather: animal skin that has been tanned and softened so it can be made into clothing, shoes, and other useful items

osnaburg: a cheap cotton fabric, originally from Germany, used to make clothes in colonial times

pelt: the skin of an animal with its hair, wool, or fur still attached

petticoat: an underskirt worn beneath a dress or an overskirt. Colonial women usually wore several layers of petticoats.

pumpkin breeches: men's pants stuffed with rags, horsehair, or sacks of grain. The stuffing was designed to make the wearer's legs look more muscular.

sampler: a piece of fabric decorated with embroidery and other stitchery. Colonial girls made samplers to practice sewing.

sempstress: a colonial-era seamstress or dressmaker

slashes: slits cut into the sleeves or other parts of a garment to show off fancy layers of fabric underneath

stay: a tight vest that colonial people, especially women, wore to improve their posture; later called a corset. The garment contained a series of wooden or whalebone rods, to provide stiffness.

swaddle: to wrap a baby tightly in a long strip of cloth. Colonial parents swaddled babies to keep them snug and to limit their movement.

tan: using chemicals to turn raw animal hide into leather. In colonial days, tanners used chemicals from deer brains for tanning.

tricorne: a wide-brimmed men's hat with the brim turned up in three places

waistcoat: a man's waist-length vest, worn alone or under a coat or a jacket

SOURCE NOTES

12 Lee Cotton, "Powhatan Indian Lifeways, Historic Jamestowne, July 1999, http://www.nps.gov/jame/historyculture/powhatan-indian-lifeways.htm (March 29, 2011).

21 Elizabeth McClellan, *History of American Costume* (New York: Tudor Publishing Company, 1969), 183.

22 Edward G. Gray, *Colonial America: A History in Documents* (Oxford: Oxford University Press, 2003), 94.

27 McClellan, *History of American Costume*, 36.

26 Linda Baumgarten, *What Clothes Reveal: The Language of Clothing in Colonial and Federal America* (Williamsburg, VA: Colonial Williamsburg Foundation, 2002), 116.

28 Ibid., 64.

30 Leslie Sills, *From Rags to Riches: A History of Girls' Clothing in America* (New York: Holiday House, 2005), 10.

33 Fisher, Leonard Everett, *The Wigmakers: Colonial Craftsmen* (New York: Benchmark Books, 2000), 18.

38–39 McClellan, *History of American Costume*, 65.

39 Ibid., 153.

47 Baumgarten, *What Clothes Reveal*, 93.

49 McClellan, *History of American Costume*, 187.

49 Ibid., 105.

51 "The Evolution of the Uniform," U.S. Army Quartermaster Foundation, March 2007, http://www.qmfound.com/uniform_evolution.htm (March 29, 2011).

SELECTED BIBLIOGRAPHY

Baumgarten, Linda. *What Clothes Reveal: The Language of Clothing in Colonial and Federal America*. Williamsburg, VA: Colonial Williamsburg Foundation, 2002.

Brasser, Theodore. *Native American Clothing: An Illustrated History*. Buffalo: Firefly Books, 2009.

Brinkley, Douglas. *American Heritage: History of the United States*. New York: Viking, 1998.

Cobrin, Harry A. *The Men's Clothing Industry: Colonial through Modern Times*. New York: Fairchild Publications, 1970.

Fisher, Leonard Everett. *The Wigmakers: Colonial Craftsmen*. New York: Benchmark Books, 2000.

Gray, Edward G. *Colonial America: A History in Documents*. Oxford: Oxford University Press, 2003.

King, David C. *First People: An Illustrated History of American Indians*. New York: DK Publishing, 2008.

McClellan, Elizabeth. *History of American Costume*. New York: Tudor Publishing Company, 1969.

Polk, William R. *The Birth of America: From Before Columbus to the Revolution*. New York: HarperCollins, 2006.

Roberts, J. M. *Modern History: From the European Age to the New Global Era*. London: Duncan Baird Publishers, 2007.

Wills, Chuck. *Destination America: The People and Cultures That Created a Nation*. New York: DK, 2005.

Zinn, Howard, and Anthony Arnove. *Voices of a People's History of the United States*. New York: Seven Stories Press, 2004.

FURTHER READING AND WEBSITES

BOOKS

Bix, Cynthia Overbeck. *Petticoats and Frock Coats: Revolution and Victorian-Age Fashions from the 1770s to the 1860s*. Minneapolis: Twenty-First Century Books, 2012.
Bix provides a fascinating overview of American fashions in the era following the colonial period.

Day, Nancy. *Your Travel Guide to Colonial America*. Minneapolis: Lerner Publications Company, 2001.
Day gives an overview of everyday life in colonial America, including descriptions of what colonists wore.

Hoobler, Dorothy, and Thomas Hoobler. *Vanity Rules: A History of American Fashion and Beauty*. Brookfield, CT: Twenty-First Century Books, 2000.
This title chronicles fashion through American history, beginning with Native Americans and the colonial era and continuing up to the twenty-first century. The emphasis is not on clothing basics but on adornments such as makeup and hairdos.

Keoke, Emory Dean. *Buildings, Clothing, and Art*. New York: Facts on File, 2005.
This book examines the contributions that native North and South Americans have made to fashion, architecture, and the arts.

Miller, Brandon Marie. *Growing Up in a New World: 1607 to 1775*. Minneapolis: Lerner Publications Company, 2003.
Journey back in time to find out what life was like for young people in colonial America. Miller discusses clothing and other aspects of daily life.

Sills, Leslie. *From Rags to Riches: A History of Girls' Clothing in America*, New York: Holiday House, 2005.
In the early colonial era, girls dressed like their mothers. But over the course of U.S. history, girls' clothing got looser and more comfortable. This book traces the changes.

Steer, Deirdre Clancy. *Colonial America*. New York: Chelsea House, 2009.
Learn more about the colonial era and its fashions in this title for young readers.

Williams, Colleen. *What the Native Americans Wore*. Philadelphia: Mason Crest, 2002.
Organized by region, this book examines Native American clothing traditions.

Winters, Kay. *Colonial Voices: Hear Them Speak*. New York: Dutton Children's Books, 2008.
Winters presents the perspectives of a variety of colonial Bostonians, from a printer and a school mistress to a baker and a shoemaker.

WEBSITES

Eighteenth-Century Clothing
http://www.history.org/history/clothing/intro/
This website from Colonial Williamsburg offers
extensive information on colonial clothing. Visitors
can learn about hats, shoes, and other accessories;
slave clothing; and the garments of wealthy men
and women. Visitors can even use an interactive
feature to dress different colonial people.

Eighteenth-Century Samplers at Pilgrim Hall
Museum
http://www.pilgrimhall.org/samplers3.htm
Here you can see authentic colonial-era samplers
and learn about the girls who created them.

What to Wear in the Seventeenth Century
http://www.plimoth.org/kids/homeworkHelp/
clothing.php
At Plimoth Plantation, a living history museum,
visitors can learn what life was like for the
Wampanoag Indians and Plymouth colonists.
The museum's website offers this page devoted
to the clothing of the British colonists and the
Wampanoag people.

VIDEOS

Colonial Williamsburg Multimedia
http://www.history.org/media/videoplayer/index
.cfm
Colonial Williamsburg offers a series of video clips
about colonial American history and culture. Several
of the videos, such as "Crafting a Colonial Ballgown"
and "Costuming the Historic Area," explain how
modern costumers re-create colonial-era clothing
for historic reenactors.

LERNER
e
SOURCE

Expand learning beyond the printed book. Download free, complementary
educational resources for this book from our website, www.lerneresource.com.

INDEX

ABOUT THE AUTHOR

Kate Havelin has written more than a dozen books for young people, including biographies of Queen Elizabeth I, Ulysses Grant, and Che Guevara. The Amelia Bloomer Project included her *Victoria Woodhull: Fearless Feminist* in its recommended list of books. Havelin has also written two trail guidebooks for adults, *Minnesota Running Trails: Dirt, Gravel, Rocks and Roots* and *Best Hikes of the Twin Cities*, both of which received awards from the Midwest Book Awards. When she's not writing, she likes to read, run, hike, kayak, ski, or snowshoe. Havelin lives in Saint Paul, Minnesota, with her husband and two teenage sons. You can visit her website, www.katehavelin.com.

PHOTO ACKNOWLEDGMENTS

The images in this book are used with the permission of: © Jameswimsel/Dreamstime.com, pp. 1, 56; © Virginia Historical Society, Richmond, Virginia, USA/The Bridgeman Art Library, p. 3; © Hulton Archive/Getty Images, pp. 4, 18, 21, 23 (top), 50; © Apic/Hulton Archive/Getty Images, p. 5; © Marilyn Angel Wynn/Nativestock.com/Getty Images, pp. 6 (top), 13 (bottom); © Marilyn Angel Wynn/Nativestock.com, p. 6 (bottom); © Atwater Kent Museum of Philadelphia/Courtesy of the Historical Society of Pennsylvania Collection/The Bridgeman Art Library, pp. 7, 36 (middle); © The Bridgeman Art Library/Getty Images, p. 8 (left); The Art Archive/Thomas Marquis Collection/Buffalo Bill Historical Center, Cody, Wyoming, p. 8 (right); Library of Congress, pp. 9 (LC-USZ62-112265), 10 (bottom, LC-USZ62-46903), 14 (top, LC-USZ62-111571), 28 (bottom, LC-DIG-pga-02417), 51 (LC-USZC4-2135), 52 (LC-DIG-pga-01591); Courtesy of the Peabody Museum of Archaeology and Ethnology, Harvard University, 90-17-50/49302 (digital file #47150009), p. 10 (top); © The Trustees of The British Museum/Art Resource, NY, p. 11 (left); The Granger Collection, New York, pp. 11 (right), 16, 26, 30, 44 (left), 47, 48, 55; © Werner Forman/CORBIS, pp. 12, 13 (top); © MPI/Archive Photos/Getty Images, p. 14 (bottom); © Peter Newark American Pictures/The Bridgeman Art Library, pp. 15, 33 (left); © Harold M. Lambert/Kean Collection/Archive Photos/Getty Images, p. 17; © SuperStock/SuperStock, p. 19; © Museum of London, UK/The Bridgeman Art Library, pp. 20 (top), 40 (right); © The Print Collector/Alamy, p. 20 (bottom); © North Wind Picture Archives/Alamy, pp. 22, 25 (bottom), 43; © Collection of the New-York Historical Society, USA/The Bridgeman Art Library, pp. 23 (bottom), 32, 35; © Frederic Lewis/Archive Photos/Getty Images, p. 24; Copley, John Singleton (1738-1815), Mrs. Jerathmael Bowers, ca. 1763, oil on canvas, 49 7/8 x 39 3/4 in. (126.7 x 101 cm), Rogers Fund, 1915 (15.128), Image copyright © The Metropolitan Museum of Art/Art Resource, NY, p. 25 (top); © Brooklyn Museum of Art, New York, USA/The Bridgeman Art Library, p. 27; © Worcester Art Museum, Massachusetts, USA/The Bridgeman Art Library, pp. 28 (top), 29; © Todd Strand/Independent Picture Service, p. 31 (top); Johnson, Joshua (fl. c. 1789-1832), Edward and Sarah Rutter, ca. 1805, oil on canvas, 36 x 32 in. (91.4 x 81.3 cm), Gift of Edgar William and Bernice Chrysler Garbisch, 1965 (65.254.3), Image copyright © The Metropolitan Museum of Art/Art Resource, NY, p. 31 (bottom); © Private Collection/The Bridgeman Art Library, pp. 33 (right), 39, 54; Photo © Christie's Images/The Bridgeman Art Library, p. 34; © Geoffrey Clements/CORBIS, p. 36 (top); © Universal Images Group/Hulton Archive/Getty Images, p. 36 (bottom); © Chris Howes/Wild Places Photography/Alamy, p. 37 (top); © Gary Ombler/Dorling Kindersley/Getty Images, p. 37 (bottom); Shoes, 17th century, silk, leather, length: 10 in. (25.4 cm), Rogers Fund, 1906 (06.1344a, b), Image copyright © The Metropolitan Museum of Art/Art Resource, NY, p. 38 (top); © Museum of Fine Arts, Houston, Texas, USA/The Bayou Bend Collection, gift of Miss Ima Hogg/The Bridgeman Art Library, p. 38 (bottom); © Cooper-Hewitt, National Design Museum, Smithsonian Institution/Art Resource, NY, p. 40 (left); © Harvard Portrait Collection, Harvard University, Cambridge, MA/Bequest of Ward Nicholas Boylston, 1828/The Bridgeman Art Library, p. 41; © Stock Montage/Archive Photos/Getty Images, pp. 42, 53; © iStockphoto.com/Laura Stone, p. 44 (right); © Science and Society/SuperStock, p. 45; © akg-images/The Image Works, p. 46; Photography Collection, Miriam and Ira D. Wallach Division of Art, Prints and Photographs, The New York Public Library, Astor, Lenox and Tilden Foundations, p. 49.

Front cover: Library of Congress (LC-USZ62-106267). Back cover: The Granger Collection, New York.

Main body text provided by Mixage ITC Book 10/15
Typeface provided by International Typeface Corp